C000148309

Waldegrave's Tales and Poetry

Waldegrave's Tales and Poetry

Kevin Waldegrave

Copyright © 2021 by Kevin Waldegrave.

ISBN: Hardcover   978-1-6641-0295-8
               Softcover   978-1-6641-0294-1
               eBook   978-1-6641-0296-5

All rights reserved. No part of this book may be reproduced or transmitted in any form or by any means, electronic or mechanical, including photocopying, recording, or by any information storage and retrieval system, without permission in writing from the copyright owner.

This is a work of fiction. Names, characters, places and incidents either are the product of the author's imagination or are used fictitiously, and any resemblance to any actual persons, living or dead, events, or locales is entirely coincidental.

Any people depicted in stock imagery provided by Getty Images are models, and such images are being used for illustrative purposes only.
Certain stock imagery © Getty Images.

Print information available on the last page.

Rev. date: 12/28/2020

To order additional copies of this book, contact:
Xlibris
AU TFN: 1 800 844 927 (Toll Free inside Australia)
AU Local: 0283 108 187 (+61 2 8310 8187 from outside Australia)
www.Xlibris.com.au
Orders@Xlibris.com.au
814118

Contents

Summer Ploughman.

The old man paused, wiped the sweat from his brow, on a sleeve of his old blue shirt, his eyes screwed up in his time weathered face, from the glare of the hot summer sun.

The mare looked around, her large hooves scuffed the ground, as if wondering at the delay, the field was long and each step you pull strong, lines as straight as a furrow should be.

Now old Tom believed that the old ways were best, and his horse was a comrade for life, a well-kept plough and a strong pair of boots were needed, with a hand that was steady and true.

He now pushed back at his ragged hat, and slowly he scratched, at his head, the summer sun struck his thick greying hair, as he thoughtfully mused on days past.

He loved the feel of the sun and the rain, and birds flying high above, they craved his land, for a road they did say, can't they wait till an old man is dead.

The sun dipped low as they finished the row, sudden pain made Tom stagger his step, he clutched the plough, his hand tight on the reins, as faithful Bessie, stood still in hers tracks.

They found him there at the end of the day, his tired eyes on the journey ahead, one foot outstretched and one in the furrow, as the shadows of summer fell really low, no more would he plough summer seed.

A Promise;

"A promise is a sacred thing, always kept, the joys to bring,

Once broken sorrows start, brings at home a broken heart."

"Never make a promise can't keep, better never spoken, than never ever kept."

Tomorrows Yesterday;

The aged hands that succoured to me, were lined and worn with care, both trembling now and hesitant, outstretched to welcome me.

The voice was soft and faintly spoke, of times now long ago, the smile was sweet and full of love, and eyes showed a heart of aglow.

I took the hands held out to me, and gently held them close, I listened long with tenderness of things that had to be.

No word was said of loneliness, nor years without a sign of those who grew up in this house, of times when she would pine.

The thin white hair and weary face, alight with joy for me as we said goodbye and waved farewell, the parted tenderly.

I turned and left, and not looked back, for time had taken all, the face I loved no longer there and no more I heard her call.

I climbed the hill of life unspent, my feet on paths well-worn as I trod the road I'd feared before, and on to life's new morn.

My Dream;

"Tis glorious to be alive this day, to dream & sing at will,

to dream of walking through a field of Daffodils,

"To walk beneath the trees at noon, to pluck sweet Bluebells,

till the moon should come creeping o'er the hills,

"To kiss goodnight all the Daffodils."

Old England;

Oh, where is the England I loved, I mourned, as Highways and Freeways the country has torn, constantly searching for familiar joy.

Many the scars in the name of progress, my searching eyes overcome with distress, oh where is the England I loved, and mourned.

My eyes overbrim with each coming dawn, gone are the cobbles in villages fair covered in seal and the streets are now bare.

Tourists like maggots, swarm into view, oh where is the England I loved & knew, gone are the moorlands, sombre and bare.

Scarred with highways thrusting through thru there, oh where is the England I loved and cared, rare is the village untouched with time.

Go down to Polperro, Lands' End & Tyme, grasping hands full of greed & grime, greet you to tarry there for a time, so many pence they will get for wine.

Oh, where is the England I loved, I cared, I mourn. So much has changed as new times dawn.

Gods Searchlights;

"I gazed upon the evening sky, filled with a strange longing was I for,

    from the vaulted heavens above, were the glorious searchlights of color."

"They filled my heart with hope and joy those golden rays,

    and warmed me through for days & days."

I'm Sorry Girls;

There was a time I thought myself a mother good and true, I'd train my sons to cook and clean, and girls would say true blue.

At an early age I trained these sons, and showed them blissfully, to make their beds and tidy rooms, and had them cooking tea.

Now Peter was reliable I could always guarantee, a well-cooked meal prepared on time and served up beautifully.

His clothes were always nice and neat, his room a sight to see, the marriage chores are shared around and was this proved successfully.

The next lad was not so good as could if had to be, the meals were done if not quite raw, but dished up willingly.

His clothes were always spick and span, I had great hope in him, alas he showed as manhood came, that this was not to be.

He now remarks the marriage scene, is great for such as he, for someone else can cook and clean, I failed here dismally.

Now in the last but not the least, is mother's pride and joy, for this one could not do what's right, a truly naughty boy was he.

His room was always in a mess, his clothes all grime and torn, his saving grace was just his love, and joy in each new dawn.

All buttons gone, his shirts unironed, his meals were burnt to a crisp, with bed unmade and top drawer up with clothes kicked underneath.

I tried most hard to train these boys, they can do it if they must, but I'm sorry now for daughters new they'll have to take them now on trust.

Foxgloves;

"The clover tinted foxgloves, that in profusion grow, their scattered sweetness lingers,

their dainty petals throw, a reflection of their beauty,

"Across hillsides where they grow, God created beauty so that the world would know,

the glory of his creations, above us & below."

Lost Heritage;

The barren land lies dull & brown, it's treeless acres bare, for man has raped this land of ours, and left without a care.

There once were forests, thick & green, as far as the eye could see, refreshing rain replenished them, and streams ran fast and free.

But man came forth in sailing ships, to claim this land his own, the dark man was already here, who spent much time alone.

Most pioneers did work & sweat, as dark man watched in fear, they cut the trees and ploughed the land, and built their houses here.

As time went by and seasons changed, the white man's ways unchecked, they robbed the dark man of his land, and lost his own respect.

They dug the dirt and mined it deep, and wealthy they became, as the dark man saw his lands despoiled, this act did cause them shame.

Erode soil & treeless plains became a common sight, all rain did cease & pastures died, and on the land a blight.

Come rise my friends and do what's right, and plant again the trees, let's work together with the earth, and welcome back the breeze.

Come search the skies for signs of rain, and tend to nature's needs, do not destroy our heritage, lets rid ourselves of greed.

Forgive us for our ignorance, and let us make amends, and to each man a pride once more, with love for lands he tends.

Sight;

"I see a golden sunset, a maidens pure delight, I see the colors streaming, away

to meet the night, I see the golden glory, like the old ancient story."

"Jesus being born that lovely night, and the mist descending, from mountain tops so white,

see the moonbeams racing, to make a silvery light."

"I see the distant heavens, it was a glorious sight, for god's own angels were,

floating by so bright."

Nobody Told Me;

Nobody told me when I was a child, that the sky was blue, or that God was true, for I just Knew.

Nobody told me of wind and rain, fast river that flow, or of stars that glow, as for I just Know.

Nobody told me in faraway hills, that the eagle flew, or of the morning dew, as for I just knew.

Nobody told me of deep restless seas, with their ebb and flow, or that youth must go, for I just knew.

Nobody told me with swift passing years, that the children grew, or the hours be few, for I just knew.

Nobody told me that I would grow old, of the thoughts that slow, or that all must go, for I just knew.

My Unfinished Prayer;

"That day my friend as we went upstream, we came upon a lovely scene,

      like ruins of an ancient dream, all clothed with sweet moss green."

"And by the waters swift & deep, I had a tiny little peep,

      a mossy log low on a tree, of a broken cross it reminded me."

"She strolled away to a different place, I so still gazed into space, and murmured a prayer,

      which by gods own grace, an unfinished prayer."

To Catch a Train;

"Wait for me" I cried as I ran down the hill as fast as I can, puffs of steam and a wave of a hand, whistle blows as I slid to a stand.

"Oh, dear no" with despair in my voice, I missed the train, it left me no choice," Don't give up," a cry in my ear, "Ride with me," these words I did hear.

"Hold your hat and scramble aboard, hang on tight and trust in the lord," fast we flew the Jigger and I, heave and pull as wind whistled by.

Hat blew off and his billy-can lost, a train to catch whatever the cost, breathless now the station ahead, "Climb down there," my rescuer said.

Engine waits as I hasten aboard, with a wave of thanks, I smiled my relief and steam then outpoured and train moves off, Jigger gone, our meeting was brief.

Bluebells;

"A rippling sea of Bluebells, beneath the skies same blue but paler,

in all the woods & dells, Remember? I remember."

"No seas are painted bluer, nor skies beneath which they grow,

no melody rings truer, each time the wind duth blow."

"The sea is growing darker, for the great west wind duth blow,

ripples turn into breakers, as the wind sweeps where they grow."

Timekeeper;

Tic toc, tic toc, that wretched clock, keeps racing thru the day, no matter how I vow I cannot work that way.

My pace is slow I really know, I should keep up with time instead of dreams, the clock just screams and bring me into line.

My stubborn pen, just did a ken, this is the way to write; Tic to tic toc, that wretched clock, just makes me want to fight.

I had a thought that came to naught, though not to be unkind, I'll stop that clock it's tic & toc will drive me from my mind.

I wound it not to make it stop, and went upon my way, and it slipped my mind I need not wind, as my thoughts led me astray.

For battery charged it onward barged, a key it did not need, tic to tic toc, that wretched clock, my plan did not succeed.

I sat me down my face a frown, and conjured up anew, that wretched clock I had to stop before my top I blew.

Success at last as I moved in fast, and knocked it from the wall, tic toc, tic toc, that wretched clock, did not survive the fall.

Shepherd's Call;

"Hark I hear a shepherd's call, soft & clear by yonder fall,

Where silence reigns supreme, and bird songs fall,

"Like crystal bells in dew filled dells, that rest beside the fall.

Hark that call rings near me still, as I stand upon this hill,

"And if it be the lord's own will, I'll hear that call by yonder fall,

This evening or the next? I wonder still."

Mixed Thoughts;

Will I? Won't I have a phone, that way I need not leave my home, think how much convenience, oh no, it does not make sense.

What's it's use? I cannot see they yatter and natter constantly, party lines are all entwined the words they speak are not always kind.

Ring, clanging as I sigh, the phone bill comes and the rates are high, good news bad news its all the same, and some folks think it's just a game.

Used, the rates are not unjust as for some the telephone's a must, business deals and calls for aid, the holes are dug and cables laid.

Friends no longer visit you, with the phone connected a call will do, time we waste is often said, so cheerfully they ring instead.

The moon;

"The moon is a porthole in the sky, thru which I can see the heavens most high,

All shrouded with silvery light, tis the most glorious sight,

The moon is a porthole in the sky, the stars are the dust from roads on high,

I gaze at them with a longing sigh, of joy, of peace, of being so nigh."

Aspiring Writer;

My pen dipped low into the ink as I strove to write my name, the words lay jumbled in the page with my first attempt at fame.

The years sped by into the past and ideas began to grow, pencilled lines on paper bags, and my childish dreams let go.

Then marriage came and spoilt the plan, and nappies filled the line, I washed the dishes and swept the floor, as right now I had no time.

My growing family needs took place of dreams I yearned to spill, and I lay the paths that each must tread, my hands were never still.

Retirement came at early age as my thought returned to school, and I tended to my writing needs even though some thought me a fool.

I scratched my head and thought in vain, the teacher sparked my brain, and encouraged to write again, with the sowing of that seed.

The words I wrote upon the page seem all to turn to rhyme, as my pen just flowed with ease of hand, for now I had the time.

Corrections plus rejection came and filled my house and home, full reams of paper and empty pens, I struggled not alone.

So many authors are the same even though some will admit it not, with much practice makes it perfect, then our aim is to cop the lot.

The Drought;

"Listen to the moaning wind, outside the farm house walls,

Listen to the whinnying fear, of horses in their stalls,

The heat with crushing warmness, descends and smothers all,

The flow'rs in the garden die, and in pots along the walls,

The birds all flutter feebly, among the drooping leaves,

And the farmers in the fields, listlessly stack corn sheaves."

The hidden Door;

The freedom of my soul wanders briefly in the wilderness, and vast green bowers spread over me, as I roam there rich & free.

Swift rushing water & placid pools entangled in the vines, dim lit cliffs untouched by time thrust high, each rock sublime.

Deep mosses green hang in continuous shrouds, clothing trunks & outstretched boughs, with everlasting green, untouched by man, unseen.

Moulding-leaves form countless paths beside the whispering stream, crystal sounds of birdsong trill, now gone yet I hear them still.

My thirst is quenched in quietude enriched by timeless hours, my soul refreshed goes out once more, but closing not the Hidden Door.

The Valley of Mystery;

"Why can't I come back to thee, why is your call not for me,

All your glory I would see, In the Valley of Mystery.

I would see your splendors, sorrow in my heart you would cause,

And in my song, I would pause, in the Valley of Mystery.

And your sweet music I'd hear, your songs that to me are dear,

How I long to be near, in the Valley of Mystery."

This House;

"This house is mine," I built it with these hands, on this land on which it stands, "This house is mine."

"This land is mine," I bought with blood & sweat, the way was hard & yet "This land is mine."

"This is my home," and here my children grew, as each one left, they knew, "This was their home."

"This earth is mine," it's warmth & deep blue skies, and night as daylight dies, "This earth is mine."

"These hills are mine," endowed with forests green and the song of bird's unseen, "These hills are mine."

"The seas are mine," storm lashed or whispering sigh, the great mounds of sand left high, "The seas are mine."

"The stars are mine," and with planets thrust afar, the void beyond ajar, "All these are mine."

The Pussy-willows;

"The frosted fur buds of the willow, peep out in shy delight,

I marvel at their beauty each tip is edged with magnificent light."

"And moonbeams flicker among the branches, to glorify the night,

"Oh, wonderous birth, of things uncared for, by careless human souls."

"But God looks down upon their beauty, as each sweet bud unfolds,

"And cares for them with joy abounding, to bless poor human souls."

Alaska & the North;

I saw a cloud streaked sky last night, lit up with misty moon-light, to me t'was like the Northern Lights, I heard the distant loon.

My mind fled back to the times long gone, where silence ruled supreme, and my heart lifted with a song.

Joy pulsed within my being, at such vast horizons on did flow, as far as the eye could see, and the silence deep fulfilled my soul, edging close to me.

My heart-strings pulled, outstretching my hand, as somewhere my youth cried earnestly, somewhere, sometime this was my land, t'was here I wished to be.

In some past life this was my home, of that I am quite sure, why else would this great land alone within my heart endure.

Could I Forget;

"Could I forget, Could I forget? The bitter cruel rain, as I stood upon the hill-top,

and cried to you in vain; Turn back I pray; turn back I pray."

The cry rang from my heart but oh I knew, I knew, I knew t'was here that we must

part, down to the Valley of Darkness, unheeding my cries, down in the depths,

onwards to death, no backward glance nor sigh. Oh, to pursue this, wandering soul,

outstretch thy longing, loving arms, and make, this one broken heart hole again."

Growing Old;

Everyone loves babies and toddlers full of charm, even teenage problem lads really mean no harm.

Young mothers are smiled upon and young men admired alike, business folk are much made of and life is full of spice.

Retirement is looked forward to though sadly lacking gold, and each decade that follows them, they finally find they're old.

In nursing homes, we place them, or they sometimes live at home, in our haste to live our life we forget they are alone.

If one stops to speak to them, they cling and want us there, impatiently we pass them by when all they want is care.

That old man who wets himself or spits upon the floor, the old lady who tidies up and does not know what for.

That one that wanders too & fro and stares with deep concern, and all each wants from life that ends, is just to love & to be loved in return.

Beauty;

"I saw a flaming sky tonight, like unto Angels wings, and in the nearing dusk,

the lonely night-bird sings, the deep perfume of violets wafts in."

"The coming of night was upon us, as they peep from folded leaves, and smiling,

welcomes night, and in the sweetness of morning." Dew-drenched the look of diamonds bright, comes the breath of Springtime, all clothed in rain,

with the ambient light glistening."

New Horizon;

"You have killed my husband!" Lucille Dupine suddenly stood up, her slim body shaking, and she felt the hysteria rise within her, her voice was charged with emotion. "Oh, dear God! You have killed him! How could you!" Her clenched fists beat savagely on the desk. She collapsed onto a chair, harsh sobs tearing at her throat, almost choking her.

Dark brown hair fell about her small oval face, the neat well dressed, figure slumped in despair. "Mrs Dupine!" The surgeon looked shocked, his face tense and pale. "We have done the best that Medical Science could do!" As he pressed the buzzer for the Sister, then spoke, kindlier. "I am very sorry Mrs Dupine, but we did warn you this may happen." Lucille looked up, her brown eyes accusing and wet with tears, her face twisted in despair. "He was my h-husband," the words were wrung from her between sobs.

He pressed the buzzer again and the Sister entered. "Yes Doctor?" "Please get this medication and see Mrs Dupine has a place to rest for a while." He handed her a slip of paper. "Very well Doctor, come Mrs Dupine, there's a quiet room just along the corridor." Lucille allowed herself to be led away, sobbing desperately, leaning on the supporting arm of the Sister. As the door clicked shut, the surgeon closed his eyes, as the case had shaken him considerably, as he nervously lit a cigarette and smoked it slowly, savouring the tang, then he wearily pressed the buzzer.

"Show Mr. Dupine in, Sister." Mr. Dupine, Doctor Schmidt will see you now," as she held the door open, and smiled sympathetically as he nodded his thanks. Bernard Dupine entered the room, and waited for the Surgeon to speak. "Mr Dupine, you do realise that everything possible was done for your brother." He looked straight at the stocky middle-aged man before him. "yes Doctor, it's very hard to accept, but we know the possibility of what could happen with a second operation. Your sister-in-law has taken it very hard." "I can well imagine this, as she depended on him utterly, I will naturally do all within my power to help. May I take her home now?" "By all means, Sister will take you to her."

"Thank you, Doctor," Bernard rose from the chair and shook hands with the Surgeon and left. He found Lucille, who was much calmer now, guiding her down the hospital stairs, assisted her into the car parked nearby, then went around the other side, got in and fastened his seatbelt. "Lucille, Maria will look after the boy for a few days, it will give you time to sort things out." "No, I want them with me!" "But Lucille-""NO!" They drove home in silence, lost in private thoughts as Bernard concentrated on the traffic, and eventually they arrived at Lucille's pleasant white weatherboard house set among tall gum trees.

Maria met them at the door, and she warmly embraced her sister-in-law. "Come Lucille, I have some coffee ready>" Then she led her inside." Robby, Harry, turn down the television, it's too loud." The two boys had already been told about their father, and like most children, had to recovered from their grief. They rushed to obey and collided, and Robby, a tall dark haired eleven-year-old, knocked Harry, a thin peaky eight-year-old to the floor. He complained sniffling in an irritating way, while Robby triumphantly turned the knob. An argument followed until Lucille, unable to stand it any longer, screamed at them. "Stop it Robby, stop it Harry!" She dropped into a chair and broke into sobs, while rocking back & forth, abandoning herself to her grief and misery. Maria & Bernard glanced at each other in dismay, but let her cry to allow the storm to pass. After a short while Lucille dried her eyes and looked up, saying shakily, "I'll have that coffee now Maria." Conversation lagged for a while then, as the evening meal was being prepared, the subject of today's events cropped up. "Bernard, will you take care of everything?"

"Of course, Lucille, are you sure that Maria can't help with the boys?" "No thank you, I want us to be together." She said. Later in the evening, husband and wife prepared to leave, and Lucille showed them to the door. "You are sure you will be alright?" Maria gently touched Lucille's arm. "Don't worry, the boys and I will be perfectly alright, and we will see you tomorrow, Goodnight." They murmured their farewells and left. Sending the boys to bed, Lucille sat into the late hours watching the television, with unseeing eyes, immune to the drone of voices and noisy music, until the station closed down. Turning it of mechanically she resumed her sitting, staring into space until the early hours of the morning, finally she slept still sitting in the armchair.

At dawn a dog barked, waking Lucille who moved stiffly, and through swollen eyes looked at the time. "Too early to call the boys," she murmured to herself, "I'll make some coffee." Like an old woman she dragged her feet into the kitchen, filled the electric jug with water and switched on the power. Lucille stared out the window, as the whole world seemed to be asleep, and she felt alone, so terribly alone. Thoughts of Wilhem, her husband, came into her mind and tears stung her eyes again, "How will I manage?" she spoke aloud and her mind was in a turmoil, she had the boys to care for and educate. She knew nothing of their financial affairs, as Wilhem had always taken care of everything, even when he was sick, she'd had others to deal with her problems. Now he was gone, and she would have to stand alone.

The jug boiled, and Lucille started the dreary process of living feeling bitter and depressed. "Why should this happen to me?" she cried "What have I done to deserve this cruelty?" The coffee was forgotten as she lost herself in her misery. The boys entered the kitchen and stood silent, not knowing or understanding their mother's anguish. "Mum" Robby spoke tentatively. "Leave me alone!" Lucille cried. "Get your own breakfast!" and rushed to her room. Uneasily they found something to eat, and again something to argue about. "That was my crust, "young Harry wailed as Robby sat munching the outside piece of bread. "I beat you to it so it's mine," Robby spoke between bites. "I wanted it, it was my turn," their voices rose in spiteful anger, then Lucille suddenly appeared and slapped them both hard across the face, almost knocking them to the floor, her eyes were blazing in fury. "If you don't stop it, I will kill you, do you hear?"

The boys with fear in their eyes, looked at their mother and did not move, the table was a shamble; butter, jam and plates were scattered, cups of milk overturned, and the white liquid dripped slowly to the floor. "Clean that mess up!" The boys scrambled to obey, never in their young lives had they been treated so harshly, their mother had always been loving, vaguely allowing them to do as they pleased. Silently they looked at her not daring to speak, and she glared back at them, her face ugly in her barely controlled anger. Suddenly Lucille turned and left the room, she was overwrought, the outbreak had shocked her and she was trembling violently. Oh God she thought, I must control myself, what is happening to me. Entering her bedroom, she closed the door, and covering her face with her hands, tried desperately to control the shaking, her mind in a whirl of thoughts. Robby & Harry, left to themselves went outside, hoping to keep out of their mother's way, "Let's go play footy in the park,' Robby suggested, "Okay, but I want first kick," said Harry, "Oh alright," Robby gave in without too much thought.

Actually, he was thankful to be away from the house, and he hated the tensions and frustrations that had been their life since their father had become sick. Secretly he had been ashamed of his father, who was so different from those of his friends. Why he hadn't been able to talk let alone walk properly, now he's gone, he felt a relief, but even now the tension was still there, and why did their mother hit them like that. Glumly, Robby looked across the park and there was no-one insight except for themselves, it must still be early. "Come on Harry," Robby kicked the ball and ran after it, young Harry felt cheated. "I hate you Meany, you said I could have first kick!" "Don't be a baby, who cares," Robby continued to kick the ball, and refused to listen to the wailing of his younger brother.

Eventually the boys decided they'd had enough, and slowly walked home, they found their aunt and uncle had arrived, and their mother was in the kitchen preparing coffee. "Hello boys," Bernard spoke cheerfully, they murmured a reply, "Where have you been Robby?" Lucille spoke sharply, "Up at the park," he said. "Well you might have said where you were going, I was nearly out of my mind with worry. Sorry," he said. "Well you had better shower and get dressed, I've laid your clothes out for you, as we leave in half an hour for the service." "Do we have to go?" Robby complained. For a moment no-one spoke, too stunned for words, and Bernard rose from the chair and walked over to Robby, placing a hand on his shoulder, "Robby, we are all going to the service for your father's funeral, you have half an hour."

Robby shrugged the hand away and followed Harry to the bathroom. "Well!" Lucille was shocked. "Go easy on the boys, they don't really understand," said Bernard as he picked up his cup. "Anymore coffee?" "Yes of course Maria do you want another cup?" "thank you, Lucille, everything will settle down, you will see." The days that followed funeral gradually became a nightmare, as Lucille became more and more unable to cope. No-one outside the home had any idea of the ranting and ravings that were commonplace each day, nor of the beltings that left the two boys speechless with fear. Their schoolwork suffered, and they became pale and thin, but no one took much notice, assuming they were still upset about their father.

Lucille managed to hide her bouts of rage from Bernard and Maria on their odd visits, then, one day her violence exploded when Robby dropped a bottle of milk on the floor. "You useless animal! I'll teach you to break things!" Lucille voice rose to a scream of fury as she grabbed the first thing to hand, a heavy wooden ladling dipper, and started to beat Robby over the head. "NO! MOTHER NO!" Robby shrieked, trying to cover his head with his arms. "let me hit you, do you hear? Let me hit you, or I'll kill you!" Lucille was beside herself, her face contorted and eyes wild, her arms flailing the helpless boy, who knelt on the floor his shrieks becoming louder with each blow.

The door burst open and Maria & Bernard rushed in, as they'd heard the screams as they stopped the car outside the gate. "Lucille stop it!" commanded Bernard grabbing her arm, eventually overcoming her frantic struggling. She collapsed in a heap, sobbing hysterically unable to stop herself. "Maria, fetch a doctor urgently!" And she rushed outside to the car then quickly drove to the nearest Medical Centre. "Quickly, I need a doctor urgently, "she was visibly upset. And the desk sister looked at her calmly, "whom is it for Madam?" "My sister-in-law! I think she's gone mad!" Maria grasped the Sister's arm. "Hurry, please get someone!" "The address please." Maria gave the address, and she was shaking so much, the Sister asked someone to take care of her. A doctor left immediately and found the house as directed.

Bernard was struggling to hold Lucille, who by now was beside herself. "Okay, hold her," and the doctor prepared a needle and injected the drug into Lucille's arm, after a few moments her struggled ceased and she became unconscious. "Well, let's have the story," as he made the patient comfortable before he sat down. Bernard briefly told about his brother's death, and what had happened when they arrived this morning.

"We will have to admit her to hospital for tests, it appears like a mental breakdown, she will recover but it may take months of care, are you agreeable." "Anything to get her well again, my wife and I will take care of the boys." They turned to where the boys were cowering, both crying, as Bernard sighed and went to them placing his arms around them, he drew them close.

"Steady now boys, it's alright do you hear, it's alright, aunt Maria and I will take care of you, come on it's alright. Your mother's sick, but will get well again, come now boys, come now." "Mum?" quavered Harry. "She's sleeping now and will go to hospital for a rest, ah, here's the ambulance." A door slammed and footsteps were heard on the path outside, Bernard crossed to the door and opened it. Maria had come back with the ambulance, and she walked inside glancing anxiously at Lucille, taking the two boys within the circle of her arms, she held them close. Lucille was taken away, and at the hospital she received extensive treatment, after many months she became well again and able to cope once more with life. "You are very fortunate Lucille, to be able to speak so many languages with such fluency, why not apply for a position with QANTAS as an interpreter, anyone who enjoys people and speaks so beautifully, must have a place somewhere, you were a tremendous help with our migrants here." "Do you really think so?

Lucille was smiling, her face alive with enthusiasm, never before had she felt so self-possessed, and confident. "I most certainly do, how about me ringing and making an appointment for an interview." "Yes, please do." After a successful interview, Lucille started in her new work with pride, and soon experienced satisfaction as she assisted many travellers with their language problems. Her self-possession and capabilities soon moved her into a social whirl, where she met many fine people. At one such function, Lucille was introduced to a QANTAS flight engineer, who acknowledged her with a twinkle in his deep blue eyes, he seemed amused for some reason, and Lucille felt slightly inadequate.

"Oh Lucille, here is someone else you should meet." Thankfully, she turned away and accompanied her hostess to the other side of the room, then later glancing up, she was perturbed to notice the quizzical look of the man previously introduced. Uncomfortably, she spoke to, June Dowling, her hostess, "Whom did you say the flight engineer was?" "Oh him, that's Darian Whitaker; He's an odd one." After several casual meetings, Lucille glanced up from her desk one afternoon, to find Darian looking at her thoughtfully. And meeting her gaze, he spoke. "Will you dine with me tonight?" Lucille contemplated, her eyes searching the bronzed face of a man before her, and satisfied, she smiled. "I'd be delighted," she said, and the long weary past fled, the future, she sensed a new horizon.

Down in my Valley;

"Down in my Valley, my little green Valley, where the mosses grow and the waters flow."

God walks;

"Where the Fantails sing, and the Skylarks wing, their glorious way, at the break of day."

God walks;

"Down in my Valley, my little green Valley, walks the timid doe,"

"Which I am sure doth know."

God walks;

Looking Back;

Eagerly the small bright-eyed child skipped from one side of the deck to the other, her golden curls bouncing freely, framing her rosy-cheeked face, that was alight with interest. Her light brown eyes took in the fact that although the ship on which she was on was moving through water, there was land on both sides! Young as she was, not yet 3yr old, she realized that this was something different, and she spied a pram nearby with a baby in it and without pausing, skipped over & took hold of the pram's handle, turning the pram round & round as if to show the baby. What happened next is dimmed, as with time, one can only assume the final scene, when possibly one mother or the other took fright, as their eyes beheld the small child handling the pram. Later Minette found herself on the top deck after climbing up the companionway steps, and her elder sister, Mildred began pushing her to & fro on the swing there. "Up-down, up-down," she gleefully cried. "More, more," and all through life, Minette thrived on swings, high trees, mountains & seas, the great outdoors.

Next, looking back she was living with her sister and parents in a small 4 roomed house with a large veranda on the front, set on several acres of land, and a passage connected the back door straight through to the front. Tanks for water stood high on stands at the back of the house, and nearby a summer house made from climbing vine, became a lovely play-house. Minette used to delight in salvaging the stale or rotten eggs, where maybe a setting for chickens had failed. Taking them into her "play-house," she would start cooking, mixing the stale eggs with soil & putting them into tins, then into an imaginary oven, the smell meant nothing. When her mother found out, Minette was chastised and the rotten eggs taken from her & disposed of. Crestfallen, Minette would wander outside and look for adventures anew, wandering in the paddocks to water the ducks or fowls. Minette delighted in the rain and in her gumboots, loved to splash around in the big puddles that lay in hollows all over the paddocks, laughing at the ducks swimming around in their watery domain, now and then finding an egg they had laid.

Pet lambs were also part of the family, and it was very hard to hold a large bottle of milk with a teat on the end for the lambs to drink, Minette's small hands would clutch the bottle tightly, with her face set in determination, as the lambs sucked greedily and bunted their heads against the bottle. Their bobbed tail bouncing as fast as they drank, but oh, the lambs were lovely to cuddle, Minette would clasp her little arms around their necks & push her face into their woolly coats, loving their softness. And sometimes when they were bigger, she'd try to ride them and of course, fall off, then she would cry out, "Grab his rag, Dad," "Grab his rag," so she could try & ride once more, the rag of course was the lamb wool! Another time a lamb came in the back-door & leapt over furniture, Minette gleefully following, laughing in delight. Minette also had a black & white kitten, and she had a dolls pram, spending hours dressing the kitten in dolls clothes, then placing it in the pram, covering it carefully, then happily pushed the pram around. The kitten appeared to enjoy the game & lay quite contented in the pram, sleeping with its bonneted head on the pillow.

Minette's sister, Mildred, being 6 years older went to school, and on occasions would attempt to teach Minette how to climb the great pine trees along the track to the gate, carefully putting Minette's hands on the branches and pushing her up. At 3years old Minette quickly picked-up the idea, and happily used to swing up and down on the smaller ones, chatting like a magpie to anyone and everyone. Possibly Minette had an invisible playmate, that adults always scoffed at, but undeterred, Minette chattered on, oblivious to all except her own small world. Pigs and cows were also part of the small farm, and many times Minette would sit on the rails of the cow-shed to watch mum & dad milk the cows, and separate the milk from cream. Mum would also churn the old cream into butter, and insisting on putting buttermilk on her face to help her skin, which was inclined to freckle. Minette hated the smell of the buttermilk on her face & used to get quite angry, nor did she like being squirted with milk from the cows teat, but used to watch delightedly as the kittens used to lap the fresh warm milk that was squirted their way, white froth covering their whiskers.

Pigs had to be fed with the skim milk, and they also had pumpkins chopped up and boiled in an old copper down the paddock, and sometimes Minette tried to help chop the big pumpkins with a tomahawk, but it was hard for a little girl, and she soon grew tired of the game, wandering away back to the house. One day while her mother was feeding the pigs, Minette looked down inside her singlet to see what was tickling, but horrified she saw a spider, screaming in terror, she ran across the paddocks, her little legs covering the distance at great speed! "Mum, mum, a spider!" tears of fright running down her face, Minette grabbed at her mother, "Take it away, take it away!" Her mother looked inside Minette's singlet & found no spider. "Stop being silly, it's gone now, it must have fallen out as you ran," Unconvinced Minette peered down her singlet front again. "It was there, I saw it," she said, between sobs.

"Well its gone, so go and see if there are any eggs in the hen-house." Minette calmer now, walked back over the paddocks to the hen-house, the spider forgotten as she began to imagine finding lots of eggs. Minette had a toy duck, to take to take to bed, made by her mother, knitted in white wool, with yellow beak and feet, she loved this duck and took it to bed with her for years, comforted by its presence. But alas poor "Diggy" had many mishaps, the ever present "Jerry", was always under the bed for nocturnal emergencies, as in the days of Minette the outside loo was quite a way from the house. Poor old "Diggy", for some reason or another quite often fell into the "Jerry" and had to be rescued, washed and dried many times in its life, much to the sorrow of Minette, for she loved "Diggy" very much. Times were hard when Minette was little & her mother was always busy making things, she would churn the cream and make the butter, she then put the butter into 1lb lots with salt, packed in her bag, bottles of cream, she would get on her bike & cycle 7miles or more into the nearest town, Wanganui, there she would exchange cream & butter for flour, sugar and sometimes even sell eggs too, then home she would cycle.

The roads then being dirt, had thick gravel & stones on them which made cycling very difficult, especially with a big, 50lb bag of flour or a 70lb bag of sugar on the carrier at the back of the bike. Her father liked to go to the cricket & Minette's mother always had this white cloth handy, from memory, Minette could not remember her father ever carrying much on his bike, maybe he stayed at home to care for the animals, or was at work, when he could get some. Minette loved baking day when her mother made bread, some with currants in, and would watch carefully as her mother cut and shaped two dough-men with eyes, a nose and mouth, then wait impatiently as they were cooked, so she could have a dough-man for her very own to eat. When it was baked, she would proudly carry it outside and sit on the front steps, then pull one arm off to eat, then the other, munching happily, touching the eyes & mouth of the dough-man with her fingers, maybe talking to it between mouthfuls. The head was next to be eaten then finally the rest of the dough-man, such delights for a small child, where pleasures were made from simple things.

Afternoon sleeps were a must for Minette, although she objected most avidly, on occasions she would persuade her mother to allow her to sleep in the hay loft, and contently she would curl up in the hay and sleep. To Minette the night was full of fears, and her sister, Mildred sometimes took a delight in scaring her, when they were in bed in the dark. The few electrics lights that were there, had long strings to turn the lights on and off, and the passage to the bedroom was long and dark, sometimes they carried a candle to light the way, which cast eerie shadows on the walls. One night, as Minette pulled the string for the light in the bedroom, nothing happened, so she pulled it again and again, still nothing and she started to take fright, her mind teeming with horrible fantasies of ghosts and such, Minette ran screaming down the hall to her parents. The fear of the dark continued to pursue her throughout the years, and one night as the two sisters slept together in a double bed, there was a fearful racket of yowling and hissing on the front veranda that ran along the front of the bedroom.

Petrified Minette lay wide-eyed with fright, hardly daring to breathe, Mildred turned over in her sleep and muttered, "Ghosts". This did nothing to calm the nerves of Minette, who sat up and screamed, her mother hastened in to calm her. By now Minette was going to Sunday School, and her mother would take the two sisters to the picnics and the wonder of this sighted fancy dress parties, she would sit-up for hours late into the night to make crepe paper dresses into a daffodil for Mildred, and a Bluebell for Minette, or other types of costumes. They would go to the parties all dressed-up hoping that their dresses would be the best. There would be children dressed as Boxes, Pixies, Fairies and all kinds of things, Minette was always shy, but would love to watch. At the Sunday School Picnics, they would have races, and Minette was placed in her age group and told when the teacher said run, to run as fast as she could to where there was a rope held some distance away. Well Minette ran as fast as her legs could go and on reaching the rope, jumped right over it! No-one had told her that was not the thing to do, there was much laughter, and Minette was very embarrassed, and had to be persuaded to go and receive her winner's prize.

Later, the children were all given ice-creams, a big three-penny size! What bliss, for even a one-penny ice-cream was a rare treat, and full of happiness Minette walked slowly, taking tiny little licks of her ice-cream, trying to make this wonderful treat last. Then –DISASTER! An older child running carelessly through the crowd, jolted into Minette, and the lovely ice-cream was knocked from her hand and fell into the dirt on the ground. Minette stood in shock and stared in horror with her happiness shattered. "My lovely ice-cream," she sobbed looking at the splash of splattered ice-cream on the ground, and with no-one to console the little girl as she stood there crying, her day completely spoilt. One day Minette and her mother went to visit a neighbour on another farm, it was a fairly large farm with many cows, which were sometimes in the paddock they had to walk through, and Minette's mother was always careful then, because when cows had their calves taken from them, they became angry and would chase people and possibly hurt them.

They walked up a long track lined with large Blue-gums which smelt lovely especially when the leaves were picked and crushed and sometimes Minette would hide them in the unscrewed-top of the bras bedpost, hoping the smell would stay, but of course that was not possible when the top was screwed back on. At the neighbour's house, Minette would wander around while her mother and the neighbour Mrs Waters talked, and tired of what she could find outside, Minette walked through the house, passed the bedrooms up the hall. She passed one room, then back-tracked as something had caught her eye, on the duchess sat a little celluloid Policeman with a bright blue tunic and a bobby helmet. Fascinated, Minette crept into the room never taking her eyes off the policeman, it was love at first sight and she picked it up, holding it. Somewhere in her mind a thought stirred. "Put it back," and slowly she put it down on the duchess and turned away, as she walked out the door a new compelling force took over, turning she quickly went and took the policeman, clutching it tightly in her hand, she crept out of the room, knowing she was doing something wrong.

Undecided, she turned and went back into the room and put the policeman back where he belonged, and on leaving the room, Minette paused and looked back. She was completely lost the charm of the policeman, as she picked it up and ran outside just as her mother called her to go home, and somehow Minette managed to hide the forbidden policeman in her knickers, the elastic in the leg stopping it from falling out. When they reached home, Minette hid under her bed and played with the policeman and talked to it. But later in the afternoon Minette's mother came looking for her and found her still under the bed with the policeman, scolding her sharply, they both returned to the neighbour and the policeman was given back to the rightful owner. Poor Minette she was devastated, the lovely policeman gone and her mother very angry with her, she was bewildered at the enormity of the wrong she had done, but couldn't really understand why it was wrong, such are the lessons of life. Some visitors came from town, all dressed up & in a big shiny car!

It had a lovely running board along the side of it, like a step to get into the car, Minette stared in admiration at such a beautiful thing, but when it moved it made an awful sound. On rainy days Minette would go into the "Front Room," this was the best room for visitors, in a corner stood a high cabinet with a wireless in it, Minette used to take her teddy & a couple of other cloth dolls, sitting behind the wireless & chatter away for hours, she played mostly alone but never lonely and she was very happy. Just before Minette started school, she and her mother would visit another neighbour, a Mrs. Smart who also lived on a farm, to Minette, this farm was a posh farm, with a long drive, it was a lovely house & Mrs. Smart used to cook beautiful cakes & biscuits for afternoon tea. She had a son called Alan, who was much older than Minette and the proud owner of and electric train, which ran through the house. Alan had it rigged up with lights that went on & off, and he tolerated Minette as she followed the train around, enjoying this new form of plaything, the visiting time passed quickly, and it was afternoon tea time, plates of beautiful cakes were offered to Minette, who kept saying, "No thank you".

Somehow, she knew that her mother didn't like her to be greedy, she longed to take one but kept refusing, when Minette arrived back at home, she said tearfully to her mother that she didn't have one of the nice cakes! Such are the woes of childhood. School-time came at last & Minette went with her sister to Westmere School, 2 to 3 miles away, walking each way, on the way home they would take their shoes and socks off & paddle in the ditches, looking for tadpoles. Oh, what joy to catch some & carry them home in a jam-jar, no thoughts of child molesters in those days, childhood was free from evil influences and life was simple. On Minette's first day at school a few children in her class asked if she'd like to see the "Poppy Show," puzzled, Minette nodded & they trooped off into the playground, where the swing, slides and monkey bars were. There, swinging upside down on the bars were several girls, their dresses over their heads and all their knickers showing! That was the "Poppy Show", giggling at the amazement on Minette's face, they pulled her along to play on the swings. Down further in the playground, was the dreaded Dental Nurse, her little hut held terrors, untold for little people that had to visit there.

The young faces in class all sombre when names were called out to go and see the Dental Nurse, each hoping that their name wasn't on the list, what fears of the young. Grateful for any kind of work, Minette's mother sometimes went to do for the better class in the district, and occasionally took Minette with her. Round eyed Minette would look at the beautiful gardens & houses, at one place, they had lots of horses, trotters and they were so well looked after that even when they died, there was a special ceremony, on the property where they were buried, and a name placed. Minette learned the fear of dogs, one day when playing in the yard a large Alsatian came up to the fence and stared, Minette didn't like the dog, so she broke off a switch from the hedge & climbing thru the fence, raised the switch & shouted "Go away Dog," The dog glared back and started towards Minette who saw with fright that the dog was going to come at her, she turned and in her haste fell over the wires on the fence, screaming.

When her mother came out the dog had gone, but the fright remained an inbuilt fear of dogs. There was a lake a few miles away & sometimes in the summer they would go swimming there, among the reeds, but Minette didn't like it much when the mud squeezed between her toes. One day when walking home with her mother, a car stopped to give them a ride, it was black and shiny, the lady driving must have known Minette's mother. Minette sat still as a mouse, eyes wide with wonder and couldn't believe how quiet it sounded, as they glided along. One day, Mildred & Minette were playing, their mother out milking or something, when Mildred decided to have a look in the big chest in the hall, a place forbidden by their mother, although Minette wasn't aware of this fact as yet. Carefully they opened the lid & peered inside, lots and lots of things were there, knitting wool, material, books and look at that! Minette's eyes almost popped out, "Look Mildred, what a big doll," there nestled among the wool was a large celluloid doll dressed like a baby, with knitted clothes all in blue. "Oh, isn't it beautiful," Minette breathed.

Just then they heard their mother come in the back door & quickly Mildred shut the lid of the chest & hastily told Minette not to say anything about what they had been doing, then they both went to find their mother to get something to eat. One day their mother asked them what they wanted "Father Christmas," to bring them, without even thinking inking, Minette cried excitedly," I want a doll just like the one in the big box," there was dead silence & Minette looked at her mother's angry face, and then at Mildred, who glared at her, "We were only looking," she said in a small voice. "You are very naughty girls; I have told you not to go poking around in things that don't concern you. There is no chance of you getting a doll like that now, "Father Christmas" will be very angry!" Minette walked slowly away, hurt that her mother was so angry, and upset to think she would never get such a beautiful doll, she rubbed the tears from her face & went and hid with her teddy, under the bed. She was wondering why her mother didn't love her anymore, as in her young mind angry people didn't love, and months later the incident was forgotten.

Christmas came & excitedly Minette looked at the foot of her bed and found a pillowslip in which were all sorts of lovely things, a new dress, black shoes with side buttons that needed a button hook to do them up. Sweets, nuts, fruit and Joy of Joys, a small china doll, about nine inches tall with long hair and a pretty dress, its eyes opened and shut, Minette was very happy. Later as she was playing with her doll, out on the veranda, Mildred asked to see the doll, Minette held it out for Mildred to take trustingly. Mildred reached out as if to take it & thinking that Mildred had hold of it, Minette let go and it smashed to the floor, broken, and Minette wept bitterly a feeling of betrayal sweeping thru her. "You dropped my dolly," she sobbed, "I did not, you did," Mildred declared, "Yes you did, I thought you had hold of it, it was an accident, tis only a doll," Mildred lost interest and moved away, as their mother came out to see what the commotion was all about, Minette sat sobbing, looking at her beloved doll. "How did you break that?" her mother asked crossly, for the doll had cost her plenty and she had very little money for such things, "Mildred dropped it," she sobbed, "I did not," Mildred cried, "she dropped it herself."

"Oh well, whatever happened it's finished with now," & she picked up the broken china & took them away, saying, "Do stop snivelling Minette, it won't bring you another." Minette just sat there crying quietly to herself, her little heart heavy, there was no anger in her thoughts to Mildred, just unhappiness. One day they had a special time at school, it was called "Pets Day", and each child could bring a pet to school, Mildred had a pet rabbit, with long white fur, and Minette a little pet lamb. Off to school they went, the rabbit in a basket with a ribbon around its neck, and Minette plodded along with her pet lamb on a rope, also with a ribbon around its neck, the lamb pranced & ran, almost pulling Minette over several times, but she hung on with both hands, and she eventually arrived at school, hot but triumphant, someone tied the lamb up to a post, for her until it was pet parade time. Minette could hardly wait, the bell rang & the children all lined up for roll call. "Children, as you know, today is Pet Day, & as soon as we have finished calling your names, go with your class to line up with your pets."

Excitedly the children fidgeted as each name was called and ticked on the roll, when it had finished, they ran to their pets, dragging, pulling or carrying them, and joining their class. The pets were not unmoved by all the excitement and started barking as they saw the cats, and the cats hissed, struggling to get out of their owner's arms. Pet calves escaped and ran around the playground, with dogs chasing them, the children trying to catch them again. Minette plonked on the ground, her arms tight around her lamb, she was determined her lamb wouldn't get away, although it's sharp hooves, hurt he legs as it moved fitfully. Eventually the teachers helped gather the animals and order was restored for a while, calm now these children paraded their pets in a circle, each proudly thinking theirs was best. Special ribbons were put on the winners, a pretty dark-eyed heifer calf with dainty legs had a ribbon added to its own, it belonged to one of the older girls. Next a collie dog with long shiny hair received her ribbon, Lady was her name, she belonged to a big freckle-faced boy.

Someone had a cockatoo, another a budgie, a sleepy Persian cat took a prize and now guess who – Minette's little lamb also had a prize, and she felt as if she would burst with happiness, Mildred sulked because her rabbit only got a third prize. After all the excitement had died down, the animals, ponies, calves, pet lambs were put in a paddock close-by and the dogs were tied up, but the cats were allowed in the classrooms where they slept, the birds & rabbits were kept in their cages on the porch until school was over, what an exciting day we had.

T'was Love;

"I lost a laugh and found a sigh, when I saw that love passed me by, yes,

t'was love, that laughing found me, alone as I wandered by yon sea."

"How sweet, that love, how pure & true, kissed at evening & at morn by dew,

the sunlight rays lingered longest, when we as one, met, loved & were blessed."

Be Still;

"Be still, & know that I am here, come rest awhile upon this fallen log,

let the stillness around you flow, and you're here."

"Within you more peaceful grows, for every bird within its bower,

they each, have loves most tender care."

"Be still, be still & know that you are one with nature, oh, can't you see,

and feel your heart more tender growing."

"Can't you see life's desert streams gentler flowing, this peace is yours,

If you rest upon this log, be still, be still & know that it's true."

Time;

"Time is but a moment of swiftly passing years,

    "Leaving naught, but mem'ries of all, the joys & tears,

"Things that happened yesterday, where only time has been,

    "Seems like an eternity, lies there in between,

"Time is passing, year by year you're growing older,

    "Time will harden, day by day you'll get colder,

"The heavens call you at morning, & with the setting sun,

    "You say, there's time for that, when all life's joys are won,

"Oh, listen my dear one, though all life's joys are won,

    "What will you be offering, when that day shall come,

"Treasures are no good, for only time, will be,

    "So why not build your treasures for all eternity."

Mother Dear;

"Your hair has turned to silver, my mother dear, as time has wrought you ailing,

from year to year the Autumn leaves are falling."

"Who will reign supreme, with the coming of spring; Tho your soul grows weary

with time, you'll be going where the sun will always shine."

"The lord I am sure has blessed you thro the passing years,

there are times I know, when he's cast away your fears,

"I know that I can leave you, as I know you'll be in his care,

but mother dear, with you there's none I can compare,

"So goodbye & God Bless you darling, mother dear,

"he, who has kept you going will ever be near,

"Until we meet again, mother dear,"

"Adieu."

Understanding;

"Oh, the puzzle of understanding, a dark veil seems to be ever hanging,

things explained but never understood, "Please understand," I wish I could."

"Only the brilliant can truly understand, the trials & troubles from day to day,

And will gently smooth them over with time, so "Trust thyself all the way.""

The Dumb;

"I see the river flowing, glinting through the trees,

"I smell the honeysuckle, wafting on the breeze,

"I hear the voices of children laughing all day long."

"I hear the sound of music, and the Thrushes song,

"I see trees, there arms upraised, and the mountain peaks."

"Oh, that I could but wonder of beauty this speaks,

"And to tell of their stature, but I'm dumb, I cannot speak."

Hushed Lies the Valley;

"Hushed lies the Valley where life's rivers flow,

"Drinking the sweetness of rain on its brow,

"No bird calls it's mate, nor trees whisper low."

"Naught but the river which thunders below,

"Hushed are our hearts midst the turmoil of years,

"Gone are the worries, sorrows & tears."

"No more of those things we all sometimes fear,

"Naught but the sweet sound, of nature we hear."

T' is Love;

"What can there be more perfect than a flushing dawn",

"There's Love, There's Love!"

"What can there be more lasting, than all of time that's born",

"There's Love, There's Love!"

"What was it that made Jesus, hang and suffer there."

"T'was Love, T'was Love!"

"What makes you go on trusting, when your life despair."

"T'is Love, T'is Love!"

"What makes us go on giving, then to give again."

"T'is Love, T'is Love!"

"What makes us grow more patient, thro' sorrow & pain,"

"T'is Love, Just Love!"

Pipe Dream;

In the shadows of the evening, I always dream of someone, who'll come along to me some day, she will be so sweet and charming and for me one thought alone, to brighten up my skies of grey.

Although it is a pipe dream, one day it may come true, and when it does my life will seem, like spring the whole year through, but as the years go drifting by now, and I go tagging along, in the smoke of this pipe dream is a distant unfinished song.

"Adieu."

Humour and Psychology;

In an interview, Phyllis Diller was asked this question; "Are you going to

follow the fashion of the stars, and have your face lifted?"

Quick as lightning came the reply; "Yeah I reckon so, my face is so cracked

they started cementing bricks around it to hold it together."

In the Quietness;

In the quietness of the evening when the sun has gone to rest,

in the hush, the birds call softly, that's the time I like best,

A great glow fills my being, and my lips send forth their praise,

when I see the trees all swaying, with their leafy arms upraise.

Embarrassment;

From some strange cause unknown to me, my words all jumbled come,

to put them right and turn them around, is easier daid than sone.

The more betangled I become, my explanations cease,

they turn away with haking sheads, from me to pet some geace.

I close my wouth mitout a nord, it's safer not to say,

and hope when dorning mawns anew, change comes with dreak
of bay.

Alas the morrow lings no bruck, my mumbled efforts bring the misery of

wumbled jords, it's most embarrassment.

My treacherous tongue will not obey, and let me say rings thight,

I may as well leave all unsaid, and keep my tips lut shight.

Spring;

Tho, the sneaking winds do blow, and the raindrops often flow,

Tho, the light frost nips your toe, and you know Spring is near!

Tho winter still surrounds you, daffodils are pushing through,

Once dead, now there's life anew, Spring is near!

Now the days are growing light, now your eyes have gained their sight,

See the nodding flowers abound so bright, Spring is here!

Leisure;

What is this life if, full of care, we have no time to stand & care?

No time to stand beneath the boughs and stare as long as sheep or cows.

No time to see when woods we pass where squirrels hide their nuts in grass.

No time to see the in broad daylight, streams full of stars, like stars on a dark night.

No time to turn at beauties glance, and watch her feet, how they can dance.

No time to wait till her mouth can, enrich that smile her eyes began.

A poor life this if, full of care we have no time to stand & stare.